English/Spanish

# Picture Dictionary

## More than 325 Essential Words

Dylanna Press

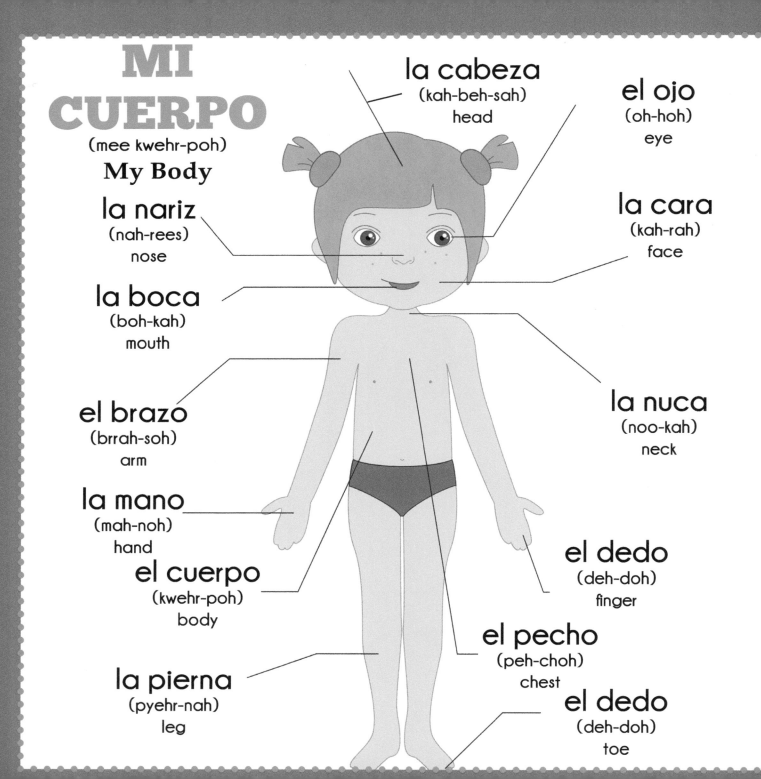

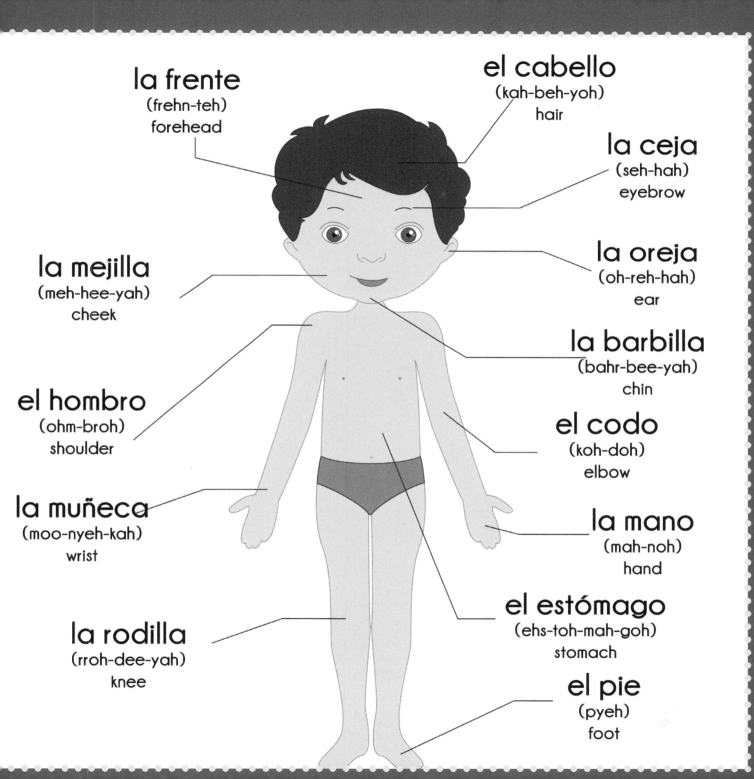

la frente
(frehn-teh)
forehead

el cabello
(kah-beh-yoh)
hair

la ceja
(seh-hah)
eyebrow

la oreja
(oh-reh-hah)
ear

la mejilla
(meh-hee-yah)
cheek

la barbilla
(bahr-bee-yah)
chin

el hombro
(ohm-broh)
shoulder

el codo
(koh-doh)
elbow

la muñeca
(moo-nyeh-kah)
wrist

la mano
(mah-noh)
hand

la rodilla
(rroh-dee-yah)
knee

el estómago
(ehs-toh-mah-goh)
stomach

el pie
(pyeh)
foot

# LA FAMILIA

(fah-mee-lyah)

Family

**el hermano**
(ehr-mah-noh)
brother

**la mamá**
(mah-mah)
mother

**el abuelo**
(ah-bweh-loh)
grandfather

**la abuela**
(ah-bweh-lah)
grandmother

**el tío**
(tee-oh)
uncle

**la tía**
(tee-ah)
aunt

**la hermana**
(ehr-mah-nah)
sister

**el papá**
(pah-pah)
father

**la prima**
(pree-mah)
cousin

**el primo**
(pree-moh)
cousin

# MI CASA
(kah-sah)

my house

## la sala de estar
(sah-lah deh ehs-tahr)

living room

## la cocina
(koh-see-nah)

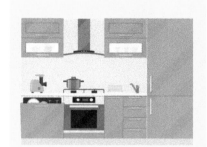

kitchen

## el cuarto
(kwahr-toh)

bedroom

## el baño
(bah-nyoh)

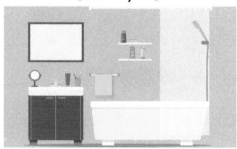

bathroom

## las escaleras
(ehs-kah-leh-rahs)

stairs

## la ventana
(behn-tah-nah)

window

## la chimenea
(chee-meh-neh-ah)

fireplace

## la puerta
(pwehr-tah)

door

## el sofá
### (so-fuh)

couch

## la silla
### (see-yah)

chair

## la mesa
### (meh-sah)

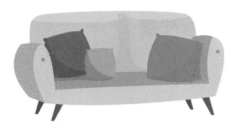

table

## la lámpara
### (lahm-pah-rah)

lamp

## el televisor
### (teh-leh-bee-sohr)

television

## la cómoda
### (koh-moh-dah)

dresser

## el escritorio
### (ehs-kree-toh-ryoh)

desk

## la biblioteca
### (bee-blyoh-teh-kah)

bookcase

## el taburete
### (tah-boo-reh-teh)

stool

# EN EL DORMITORIO

(ehn ehl
dohr-mee-toh-ryoh)

## In the bedroom

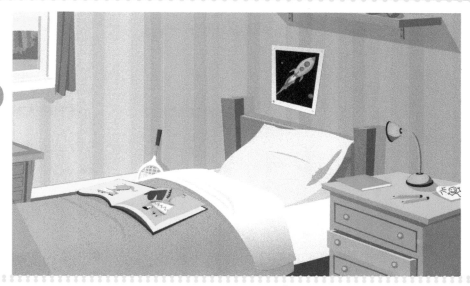

## la cama
(kah-mah)

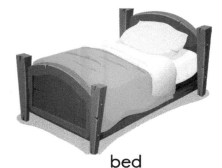

bed

## la almohada
(ahl-moh-ah-dah)

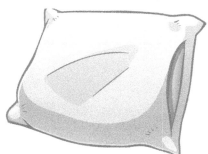

pillow

## la manta
(mahn-tah)

blanket

## el armario
(ahr-mah-ryoh)

wardrobe

## el reloj
(rreh-lohh)

clock

## el espejo
(ehs-peh-hoh)

mirror

# LA COCINA
### (koh-see-nah)

kitchen

## la nevera
### (neh-beh-rah)

refrigerator

## la estufa
### (ehs-too-fah)

stove

## el tazón
### (tah-sohn)

bowl

## la taza
### (tah-sah)

cup

## el vaso
### (bah-soh)

glass

## la tabla de cortar
### (tah-blah deh kohr-tahr)

cutting board

## el cuchillo
### (koo-chee-yoh)

knife

## el tenedor
### (teh-neh-dohr)

fork

## el hervidor
(ehr-bee-dohr)

kettle

## la sartén
(sahr-tehn)

pan

## la olla
(oh-yah)

pot

## el plato
(plah-toh)

plate

## la cuchara
(koo-chah-rah)

spoon

## la tetera
(teh-teh-rah)

teapot

## el batidor
(bah-tee-dohr)

whisk

## el lavavajillas
(lah-bah-bah-hee-yahs)

dishwasher

## el microondas
(mee-kroh-ohn-dahs)

microwave

# EL BAÑO
(bah-nyoh)

bathroom

## la bañera
(bah-nyeh-rah)

bathtub

## el jabón
(hah-bohn)

soap

## el cepillo
(seh-pee-yoh)

brush

## las burbujas
(boor-boo-hahs)

bubbles

## la peinilla
(pey-nee-yah)

comb

## la llave
(yah-beh)

faucet

## la báscula
(bahs-koo-lah)

scale

## el champú
(chahm-poo)

shampoo

# la ducha
### (doo-chah)

shower

# el lavabo
### (lah-bah-boh)

sink

# la esponja
### (ehs-pohn-hah)

sponge

# el pañuelo
### (pah-nyweh-loh)

tissue

# el inodoro
### (ee-noh-doh-roh)

toilet

# el cepillo de dientes
### (seh-pee-yoh deh dyehn-tehs)

toothbrush

# la pasta de dientes
### (pahs-tah deh dyehn-tehs)

toothpaste

# la toalla
### (toh-ah-yah)

towel

# el papel higiénico
### (pah-pehl ee-hyeh-nee-koh)

toilet paper

# MI ROPA
(rroh-pah)

My Clothes

## el cinturón
(seen-too-rohn)

## el traje de baño
(trah-heh deh bah-nyoh)

## la blusa
(blaus)

belt

swimsuit

blouse

## la bota
(boh-tah)

## el abrigo
(ah-bree-goh)

## el vestido
(behs-tee-doh)

boots

coat

dress

## el guante
(gwahn-teh)

## la chaqueta
(chah-keh-tah)

## el gorro
(goh-rroh)

gloves

jacket

hat

## los vaqueros
(bah-keh-rohs)

jeans

## la corbata
(kohr-bah-tah)

necktie

## los pantalones
(pahn-tah-lohn-ehs)

pants

## el overol
(oh-beh-rohl)

overalls

## la cartera
(kahr-teh-rah)

purse

## el pijama
(pee-yah-mah)

pajamas

## la bufanda
(boo-fahn-dah)

scarf

## la ropa interior
(rroh-pah een-teh-ryohr)

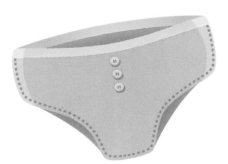

underwear

## los zapatos
(sah-pah-tohs)

shoes

## la falda
(fahl-dah)

skirt

## los tenis
(teh-nees)

sneakers

## los calcetines
(kahl-seh-teen-ehs)

socks

## las gafas de sol
(gah-fahs deh sohl)

sunglasses

## el suéter
(sweh-tehr)

sweater

## la camiseta
(kah-mee-seh-tah)

T shirt

## las mallas
(mah-yahs)

tights

## el traje de baño
(trah-heh deh bah-nyoh)

swim trunks

## la sudadera
(soo-dah-deh-rah)

sweatshirt

# LA COMIDA
(koh-mee-dah)

Food

## el tomate
(toh-mah-teh)

tomato

## la sandía
(sahn-dee-ah)

watermelon

## la manzana
(mahn-sah-nah)

apple

## la naranja
(nah-rahng-hah)

orange

## el plátano
(plah-tah-noh)

banana

## las fresas
(freh-sahs)

strawberries

## el limón
(lee-mohn)

lemon

## la pera
(peh-rah)

pear

## la ensalada
(ehn-sah-lah-dah)

salad

## el queso
keh-soh)

cheese

## el pollo
(poh-yoh)

chicken

## los comestibles
koh-mehs-tee-blehs)

groceries

## los panqueques
(pahng-keh-kehs)

pancakes

## el emparedado
(ehm-pah-reh-dah-doh)

sandwich

## el espagueti
ehs-pah-geh-tee)

spaghetti

## el pan tostado
(pahn tohs-tah-doh)

toast

## el maíz
(mah-ees)

corn

# la mantequilla
(mahn-teh-kee-yah)

butter

# el arroz
(ah-rrohs)

rice

# el pastel
(pahs-tehl)

cake

# las nueces
(nwehs-ez)

nuts

# el huevo
(weh-boh)

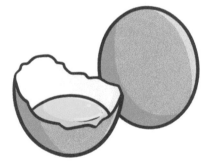

egg

# las patatas
(pah-tah-tahs)

potatoes

# el pan
(pahn)

bread

# las patatas fritas
(pah-tah-tahs free-tahs)

chips

# las galletas
(gah-yeh-tahs)

cookies

## las palomitas
(pah-loh-mee-tahs)

popcorn

## las patatas fritas
(pah-tah-tahs free-tahs)

french fries

## el helado
(eh-lah-doh)

ice cream

## la zanahoria
(sah-nah-oh-ryah)

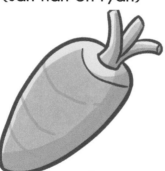

carrot

## la pizza
(pit-suh)

pizza

## el brócoli
(broh-koh-lee)

broccoli

## la leche
(leh-cheh)

milk

## la cebolla
(seh-boh-yah)

onion

## el pavo
(pah-boh)

turkey

# LOS ANIMALES
(ahn-ih-muhl-ez)

Animals

## el pájaro
(pah-hah-roh)

bird

## el gato
(gah-toh)

cat

## el perro
(peh-rroh)

dog

## el pato
(pah-toh)

duck

## el elefante
(eh-leh-fahn-teh)

elephant

## el zorro
(soh-rroh)

fox

## el pavo
(pah-boh)

turkey

## la ballena
(bah-yeh-nah)

whale

## el panda
(pahn-dah)

panda

## la rana
(rrah-nah)

frog

## el búho
boo-oh)

owl

## el conejo
(koh-neh-hoh)

rabbit

## el gallo
(gah-yoh)

rooster

## el mono
(moh-noh)

monkey

## el león
(leh-ohn)

lion

## el alce
(ahl-seh)

moose

## la ardilla
(ahr-dee-yah)

squirrel

## la serpiente
(sehr-pyehn-teh)

snake

## el ratón
(rrah-tohn)

mouse

## el pollo
(poh-yoh)

chicken

## el caimán
(kay-mahn)

alligator

## el oso
(oh-soh)

bear

# el cerdo
### (sehr-doh)

pig

# la tortuga
### (tohr-too-gah)

turtle

# el hipopótamo
### (ee-poh-poh-tah-moh)

hippopotamus

# la jirafa
### (hee-rah-fah)

giraffe

# el camello
### (kah-meh-yoh)

camel

# el lobo
### (loh-boh)

wolf

# la cebra
### (seh-brah)

zebra

# el pez
### (pehs)

fish

# la vaca
### (bah-kah)

cow

# la oveja
### (oh-beh-hah)

sheep

## la cabra
### (kah-brah)

goat

## el caballo
### (kah-bah-yoh)

horse

## el tigre
### (tee-greh)

tiger

## el caracol
### (kah-rah-kohl)

snail

## el pingüino
### (peeng-gwee-noh)

penguin

## el gorila
### (goh-ree-lah)

gorilla

# LA ESCUELA
(ehs-kweh-lah)

## el autobús escolar
(ow-toh-boos ehs-koh-lahr)

## el profesor
(proh-feh-sohr)

school

school bus

teacher

## el crayón
(krah-yohn)

## la pega
(peh-gah)

## los cuadernos
(kwah-dehr-nohs)

crayons

glue

notebooks

## la pintura
(peen-too-rah)

## el lápiz
(lah-pees)

## el globo terráqueo
(gloh-boh teh-rrah-keh-oh)

paint

pencil

globe

## la mochila
(moh-chee-lah)

backpack

## el bolígrafo
(boh-lee-grah-foh)

pen

## la regla
(rreh-glah)

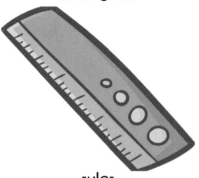

ruler

## la calculadora
(kahl-koo-lah-doh-rah)

calculator

## la tijera
(tee-heh-rah)

scissors

## la grapadora
(grah-pah-doh-rah)

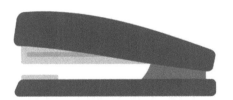

stapler

## el libro
(lee-broh)

book

## el escritorio
(ehs-kree-toh-ryoh)

desk

## la estudiante
(ehs-too-dyahn-teh)

student

# EL CLIMA
(klee-mah)

weather

## la nube
(noo-beh)

cloud

## el relámpago
(rreh-lahm-pah-goh)

lightning

## la lluvia
(yoo-byah)

rain

## la nieve
(nyeh-beh)

snow

## el sol
(sohl)

sun

## el tornado
(tohr-nah-doh)

tornado

## el viento
(byehn-toh)

wind

## el arco iris
(ahr-koh ee-rees)

rainbow

# LAS ESTACIONES - THE SEASONS

## el invierno
### (een-byehr-noh)

winter

## la primavera
### (pree-mah-beh-rah)

spring

## el verano
### (beh-rah-noh)

summer

## el otoño
### (oh-toh-nyoh)

fall

# LA TRANSPORTACIÓN
(trahns-pohr-tah-syohn)
transportation

## el avión
(ah-byohn)

airplane

## la ambulancia
(ahm-boo-lahn-syah)

ambulance

## la bicicleta
(bee-see-kleh-tah)

bicycle

## el barco
(bahr-koh)

boat

## el autobús
(ow-toh-boos)

bus

## el coche
(koh-cheh)

car

## el carro de bomberos
(kah-rroh deh bohm-beh-rohs )

firetruck

## el helicóptero
(eh-lee-kohp-teh-roh)

helicopter

## la motocicleta
(moh-toh-see-kleh-tah)

motorcycle

## la patrulla
(pah-troo-yah)

police car

## el cohete
(koh-eh-teh)

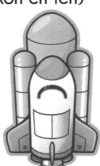

rocket

## el patinete
(pah-tee-neh-teh)

scooter

## el buque
(boo-keh)

ship

## el submarino
(soob-mah-ree-noh)

submarine

## el tractor
(trahk-tuhr)

tractor

## el tren
(trehn)

train

## el camión
(kah-myohn)

truck

## el carro
(kah-rroh)

wagon

# DEPORTES - SPORTS
(deh-pohr-tehs)

## el guante
(gwahn-teh)

glove

## la pelota de béisbol
(peh-loh-tah deh beys-bohl)

baseball

## el básquetbol
(bahs-keht-bohl)

basketball

## el monopatín
(moh-noh-pah-teen)

skateboard

## la raqueta de tenis
(boor-boo-hahs)

tennis racket

## el silbato
(seel-bah-toh)

whistle

## el boxeo
(bohk-seh-oh)

boxing

## la pesca
(pehs-kah)

fishing

## el fútbol americano
(foot-bohl ah-meh-ree-kah-noh)

football

## el golf
(gohlf)

golf

## el patinaje
(pah-tee-nah-heh)

skating

## el karate
(kah-ra-te)

karate

## el fútbol
(foot-bohl)

soccer

## la vela
(beh-lah)

sailing

## el tenis
(teh-nees)

tennis

# PALABRAS DE ACCIÓN
(pah-lah-brahs duh ahk-syohn)
Action Words

## gatear
(gah-teh-ahr)

crawl

## escalar
(ehs-kah-lahr)

climb

## llorar
(yoh-rahr)

cry

## beber
(beh-behr)

drink

## comer
(koh-mehr)

eat

## saltar
(sahl-tahr)

jump

## reírse
(rreh-eer-seh)

laugh

## escuchar
(ehs-koo-chahr)

listen

## leer
(leh-ehr)

read

## correr
### (koh-rrehr)

run

## sentarse
### (sehn-tahr-seh)

sit

## dormir
### (dohr-meer)

sleep

## de pie
### (deh pyeh)

stand

## hablar
### (ah-blahr)

talk

## caminar
### (kah-mee-nahr)

walk

## susurrar
### (soo-soo-rrahr)

whisper

## abrazar
### (ah-brah-sahr)

hug

## rebotar
### (rreh-boh-tahr)

bounce

# LAS EMOCIONES - EMOTIONS
(eh-moh-syohn-ays)

## tener miedo
(teh-nehr myeh-doh)

afraid

## curioso
(koo-ryoh-soh)

curious

## triste
(trees-teh)

sad

## enfadado
(ehm-fah-dah-doh)

angry

## sorprendido
(sohr-prehn-dee-doh)

surprised

## feliz
(feh-lees)

happy

# OPUESTOS - OPPOSITES
### (oh-pwehs-tohs)

## sucio
### (soo-syoh)

## limpio
### (leem-pyoh)

## cerrado
### (seh-rrah-doh)

## abierto
### (ah-byehr-toh)

dirty

clean

closed

open

## frío
### (free-oh)

## caliente
### (kah-lyehn-teh)

## claro
### (klah-roh)

## oscuro
### (ohs-koo-roh)

cold

hot

light

dark

# OPUESTOS - OPPOSITES

### viejo
(byeh-hoh)

### joven
(hoh-behn)

### pesado
(peh-sah-doh)

### ligero
(lee-heh-roh)

old

young

heavy

light

### fuerte
(fwehr-teh)

### tranquilo
(trahny-kee-loh)

### abajo
(ah-bah-hoh)

### arriba
(ah-rree-bah)

loud

quiet

down

up

# OPUESTOS - OPPOSITES

**seco**
(seh-koh)

**mojado**
(moh-hah-doh)

**suave**
(swah-beh)

**duro**
(doo-roh)

dry

wet

soft

hard

**tirar**
(tee-rahr)

**empujar**
(ehm-poo-hahr)

**arriba de**
(ah-rree-bah deh)

**debajo de**
(deh-bah-hoh deh)

pull

push

above

below

# FORMAS - SHAPES
(fohr-mahs)

## el círculo
(seer-koo-loh)

circle

## el rombo
(rrohm-boh)

diamond

## el rectángulo
(rrehk-tahng-goo-loh)

rectangle

## el cuadrado
(kwah-drah-doh)

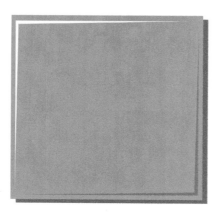

square

## la estrella
(ehs-treh-yah)

star

## el triángulo
(tryahng-goo-loh)

triangle

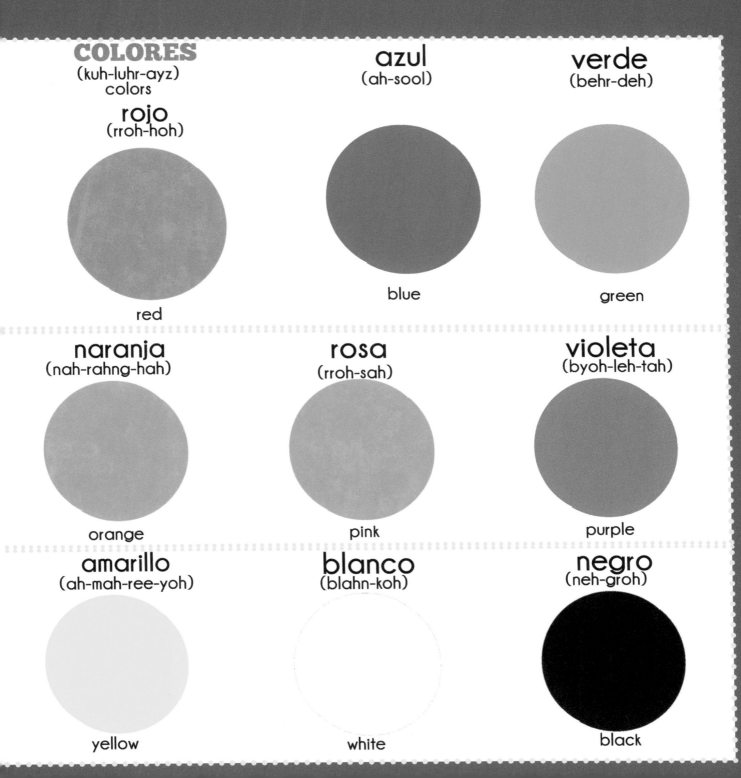

# COLORES
(kuh-luhr-ayz)
colors

## rojo
(rroh-hoh)

red

## azul
(ah-sool)

blue

## verde
(behr-deh)

green

## naranja
(nah-rahng-hah)

orange

## rosa
(rroh-sah)

pink

## violeta
(byoh-leh-tah)

purple

## amarillo
(ah-mah-ree-yoh)

yellow

## blanco
(blahn-koh)

white

## negro
(neh-groh)

black

# NÚMEROS - NUMBERS
(noo-meh-rohs)

### uno
(byeh-hoh)

### dos
(byeh-hoh)

### tres
(byeh-hoh)

### cuatro
(byeh-hoh)

### cinco
(byeh-hoh)

one

two

three

four

five

### seis
(byeh-hoh)

### siete
(byeh-hoh)

### ocho
(byeh-hoh)

### nueve
(byeh-hoh)

### diez
(byeh-hoh)

six

seven

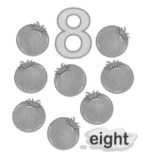
eight

nine

ten

# EL ALFABETO - ALPHABET

(ahl-fah-beh-toh)

| A | B | C | D | E | F | G | H | I |
|---|---|---|---|---|---|---|---|---|
| a | be | ce | de | e | efe | ge | hache | i |
| (ah) | (bay) | (say) | (day) | (ay) | (effay) | (hay) | (ach-ay) | (ee) |
| J | K | L | M | N | Ñ | O | P | Q |
| jota | ka | ele | eme | ene | eñe | o | pe | cu |
| (hota) | (ka) | (el-lay) | (eh-may) | (eh-nay) | (en-yay) | (o) | (pay) | (koo) |
| R | S | T | U | V | W | X | Y | Z |
| ere | ese | te | u | ve | doble ve | equis | i griega | zeta |
| (er-ay) | (es-say) | (tay) | (ooh) | (vay) | (do-blay-vay) | (ay-kees) | (e-gree-ay-ga) | (say-ta) |

# Spanish-English Word List

| | | | |
|---|---|---|---|
| abajo | down | la boca | mouth |
| abierto | open | el bolígrafo | pen |
| abrazar | hugging | la bota | boot |
| el abrigo | coat | el boxeo | boxing |
| el abuelo | grandfather | el brazo | arm |
| el alce | moose | el brócoli | broccoli |
| la almohada | pillow | la bufanda | scarf |
| amarillo | yellow | el búho | owl |
| la ambulancia | ambulance | el buque | ship |
| los animales | animals | las burbujas | bubbles |
| la arco iris | rainbow | el caballo | horse |
| la ardilla | squirrel | el cabello | hair |
| el armario | wardrobe | la cabeza | head |
| arriba | up | la cabra | goat |
| arriba de | above | el caimán | alligator |
| el arroz | rice | los calcetines | socks |
| el autobús | bus | la calculadora | calculator |
| el autobus escolar | schoolbus | caliente | hot |
| azul | blue | la cama | bed |
| la ballena | whale | el camello | camel |
| la bañera | bathtub | caminar | walking |
| el baño | bathroom | el camión | truck |
| la barbilla | chin | la camiseta | shirt |
| el barco | boat | la cara | face |
| la báscula | scale | el caracol | snail |
| el básquetbol | basketball | el carro de | |
| el batidor | whisk | bomberos | fire truck |
| beber | drinking | la cartera | purse |
| la biblioteca | library | la casa | house |
| la bicicleta | bicycle | la cebolla | onion |
| blanco | white | la cebra | zebra |
| la blusa | blouse | la ceja | eyebrow |

# Spanish-English Word List

| | | | |
|---|---|---|---|
| el cepillo | brush | de pie | standing |
| el cepillo de dientes | toothbrush | debajo de | below |
| el cerdo | pig | el dedo | finger, toe |
| cerrado | closed | los deportes | sports |
| el champú | shampoo | diez | ten |
| la chaqueta | jacket | dormir | sleeping |
| la chimenea | fireplace | el dormitorio | bedroom |
| cinco | five | dos | two |
| el círculo | circle | la ducha | shower |
| claro | light | duro | hard |
| el clima | weather | el elefante | elephant |
| el coche | car | las emociones | emotions |
| la cocina | kitchen | el emparedado | sandwich |
| la cuchara | spoon | empujar | push |
| el codo | elbow | enfadado | angry |
| el cohete | rocket | la ensalada | salad |
| los colores | colors | escalar | climbing |
| comer | eating | las escaleras | stairs |
| los comestibles | groceries | el escritorio | desk |
| la comida | food | escuchar | listening |
| la cómoda | dresser | la escuela | school |
| el conejo | rabbit | el espagueti | spaghetti |
| la corbata | necktie | el espejo | mirror |
| correr | running | la esponja | sponge |
| el crayón | crayons | las estaciones | seasons |
| los cuadernos | notebooks | el estómago | stomach |
| el cuadrado | square | la estrella | star |
| el cuarto | bedroom | la estudiante | student |
| el cuchillo | knife | la estufa | stove |
| el cuerpo | body | la falda | skirt |
| curioso | curious | la familia | family |
| | | feliz | happy |

# Spanish-English Word List

| | | | |
|---|---|---|---|
| las formas | shapes | el karate | karate |
| la frente | forehead | la lámpara | lamp |
| las fresas | strawberries | el lápiz | pencil |
| frío | cold | el lavabo | sink |
| fuerte | strong | el lavavajillas | dishwasher |
| el fútbol | soccer | la leche | milk |
| el fútbol americano | football | leer | read |
| las gafas de sol | sunglasses | el león | lion |
| las galletas | cookies | el libro | book |
| el gallo | rooster | ligero | light |
| gatear | crawling | el limón | lemon |
| el gato | cat | limpio | clean |
| el globo terráqueo | globe | la llave | faucet |
| el golf | golf | llorar | cry |
| el gorila | gorilla | la lluvia | rain |
| el gorro | hat | el lobo | wolf |
| la grapadora | stapler | el maíz | corn |
| el guante | glove | las mallas | tights |
| hablar | talking | la mamá | mother |
| el helado | ice cream | la mano | hand |
| el helicóptero | helicopter | la manta | blanket |
| la hermana | sister | la mantequilla | butter |
| el hermano | brother | la manzana | apple |
| el hervidor | kettle | la mejilla | cheek |
| el hipopótamo | hippopotamus | la mesa | table |
| el hombro | shoulder | el microondas | microwave |
| el huevo | egg | la mochila | backpack |
| el inodoro | toilet | mojado | wet |
| invierno | winter | el mono | monkey |
| el jabón | soap | el monopatín | skateboard |
| la jirafa | giraffe | la motocicleta | motorcycle |
| joven | young | la muñeca | wrist |

# Spanish-English Word List

| | | | |
|---|---|---|---|
| el naranja | orange (color) | el pastel | cake |
| la naranja | orange (fruit) | las patatas | potatoes |
| la nariz | nose | las patatas fritas | chips, french fries |
| negro | black | | |
| la nevera | refrigerator | el patinaje | skating |
| la nieve | snow | el patinete | scooter |
| la nube | cloud | el pato | duck |
| la nuca | neck | la patrulla | police car |
| las nueces | nuts | el pavo | turkey |
| nueve | nine | el pecho | chest |
| los números | numbers | la pega | glue |
| ocho | eight | la peinilla | comb |
| el ojo | eye | la pelota de béisbol | baseball |
| la olla | pot | la pera | pear |
| los opuestos | opposites | el perro | dog |
| la oreja | ear | pesado | heavy |
| oscuro | dark | la pesca | fishing |
| el oso | bear | el pez | fish |
| otoño | autumn | el pie | foot |
| la oveja | sheep | la pierna | leg |
| el overol | overalls | el pijma | pajamas |
| el pájaro | bird | el pingüino | penguin |
| las palomitas | popcorn | la pintura | paint |
| el pan | bread | la pizza | pizza |
| el pan tostado | toast | el plátano | banana |
| el panda | panda | el plato | plate |
| los panqueques | pancakes | el pollo | chicken |
| los pantalones | pants | la prima | cousin |
| el pañuelo | tissue | primavera | spring |
| el papá | father | el primo | cousin |
| el papel higiénico | toilet paper | el profesor | teacher |
| la pasta de dientes | toothpaste | la puerta | door |

# Spanish-English Word List

| | | | |
|---|---|---|---|
| el queso | cheese | sucio | dirty |
| la rana | frog | la sudadera | sweatshirt |
| la raqueta de tenis | tennis racket | el suéter | sweater |
| el ratón | mouse | susurrar | whisper |
| rebotar | bounce | la tabla de cortar | cutting board |
| el rectángulo | rectangle | el taburete | stool |
| la regla | ruler | la taza | cup |
| reírse | laugh | el tazón | bowl |
| el relámpago | lightning | el televisor | television |
| el reloj | clock | el tenedor | fork |
| la rodilla | knee | tener miedo | afraid |
| rojo | red | los tenis | sneakers |
| el rombo | diamond | la tetera | teapot |
| la ropa | clothes | la tía | aunt |
| la ropa interior | underwear | el tigre | tiger |
| rosa | pink | la tijera | scissors |
| la sala de estar | living room | el tío | uncle |
| saltar | jump | tirar | pull |
| la sandía | watermelon | la toalla | towel |
| la sartén | pan | el tomate | tomato |
| seco | dry | el tornado | tornado |
| seis | six | la tortuga | turtle |
| sentarse | sit | el tractor | tractor |
| la serpiente | snake | el traje de baño | swimsuit |
| siete | seven | tranquilo | quiet |
| el silbato | whistle | la transportación | transportation |
| la silla | chair | el tren | train |
| el sofá | couch | tres | three |
| el sol | sun | el triángulo | triangle |
| sorprendido | surprised | triste | sad |
| suave | soft | uno | one |
| el submarino | submarine | la vaca | cow |

# Spanish-English Word List

| | |
|---|---|
| **los vaqueros** | jeans |
| **el vaso** | glass |
| **la vela** | sailing |
| **la ventana** | window |
| **el verano** | summer |
| **verde** | green |
| **el vestido** | dress |
| **viejo** | old |
| **el viento** | wind |
| **violeta** | purple |
| **la zanahoria** | carrot |
| **los zapatos** | shoes |
| **el zorro** | fox |

# English-Spanish Word List

| | | | |
|---|---|---|---|
| **above** | arriba de | **bowl** | el tazón |
| **afraid** | tener miedo | **boxing** | el boxeo |
| **alligator** | el caimán | **bread** | el pan |
| **ambulance** | la ambulancia | **broccoli** | el brócoli |
| **angry** | enfadado | **brother** | el hermano |
| **animals** | los animales | **brush** | el cepillo |
| **apple** | la manzana | **bubbles** | las burbujas |
| **arm** | el brazo | **bus** | el autobús |
| **aunt** | la tía | **butter** | la mantequilla |
| **autumn** | otoño | **cake** | el pastel |
| **backpack** | la mochila | **calculator** | la calculadora |
| **banana** | el plátano | **camel** | el camello |
| **baseball** | la pelota de béisbol | **car** | el coche |
| **basketball** | el básquetbol | **carrot** | la zanahoria |
| **bathroom** | el baño | **cat** | el gato |
| **bathtub** | la bañera | **chair** | la silla |
| **bear** | el oso | **cheek** | la mejilla |
| **bed** | la cama | **cheese** | el queso |
| **bedroom** | el cuarto | **chest** | el pecho |
| **bedroom** | el dormitorio | **chicken** | el pollo |
| **below** | debajo de | **chin** | la barbilla |
| **bicycle** | la bicicleta | **chips** | las patatas fritas |
| **bird** | el pájaro | **circle** | el círculo |
| **black** | negro | **clean** | limpio |
| **blanket** | la manta | **climbing** | escalar |
| **blouse** | la blusa | **clock** | el reloj |
| **blue** | azul | **closed** | cerrado |
| **boat** | el barco | **clothes** | la ropa |
| **body** | el cuerpo | **cloud** | la nube |
| **book** | el libro | **coat** | el abrigo |
| **boot** | la bota | **cold** | frío |
| **bounce** | rebotar | **colors** | los colores |

# English-Spanish Word List

| | | | |
|---|---|---|---|
| comb | la peinilla | emotions | las emociones |
| cookies | las galletas | eye | el ojo |
| corn | el maíz | eyebrow | la ceja |
| couch | el sofá | face | la cara |
| cousin | la prima | family | la familia |
| cousin | el primo | father | el papá |
| cow | la vaca | faucet | la llave |
| crawling | gatear | finger, toe | el dedo |
| crayons | el crayón | | el carro de |
| cry | llorar | fire truck | bomberos |
| cup | la taza | fireplace | la chimenea |
| curious | curioso | fish | el pez |
| cutting board | la tabla de cortar | fishing | la pesca |
| dark | oscuro | five | cinco |
| desk | el escritorio | food | la comida |
| diamond | el rombo | foot | el pie |
| dirty | sucio | football | el fútbol americano |
| dishwasher | el lavavajillas | forehead | la frente |
| dog | el perro | fork | el tenedor |
| door | la puerta | fox | el zorro |
| down | abajo | frog | la rana |
| dress | el vestido | giraffe | la jirafa |
| dresser | la cómoda | glass | el vaso |
| drinking | beber | globe | el globo terráqueo |
| dry | seco | glove | el guante |
| duck | el pato | glue | la pega |
| ear | la oreja | goat | la cabra |
| eating | comer | golf | el golf |
| egg | el huevo | gorilla | el gorila |
| eight | ocho | grandfather | el abuelo |
| elbow | el codo | green | verde |
| elephant | el elefante | groceries | los comestibles |

# English-Spanish Word List

| | | | |
|---|---|---|---|
| hair | el cabello | living room | la sala de estar |
| hand | la mano | microwave | el microondas |
| happy | feliz | milk | la leche |
| hard | duro | mirror | el espejo |
| hat | el gorro | monkey | el mono |
| head | la cabeza | moose | el alce |
| heavy | pesado | mother | la mamá |
| helicopter | el helicóptero | motorcycle | la motocicleta |
| hippopotamus | el hipopótamo | mouse | el ratón |
| horse | el caballo | mouth | la boca |
| hot | caliente | neck | la nuca |
| house | la casa | necktie | la corbata |
| hugging | abrazar | nine | nueve |
| ice cream | el helado | nose | la nariz |
| jacket | la chaqueta | notebooks | los cuadernos |
| jeans | los vaqueros | numbers | los números |
| jump | saltar | nuts | las nueces |
| karate | el karate | old | viejo |
| kettle | el hervidor | one | uno |
| kitchen | la cocina | onion | la cebolla |
| knee | la rodilla | open | abierto |
| knife | el cuchillo | opposites | los opuestos |
| lamp | la lámpara | orange (color) | el naranja |
| laugh | reírse | orange (fruit) | la naranja |
| leg | la pierna | overalls | el overol |
| lemon | el limón | owl | el búho |
| library | la biblioteca | paint | la pintura |
| light | claro | pajamas | el pijma |
| light | ligero | pan | la sartén |
| lightning | el relámpago | pancakes | los panqueques |
| lion | el león | panda | el panda |
| listening | escuchar | pants | los pantalones |

# English-Spanish Word List

| | | | |
|---|---|---|---|
| pear | la pera | salad | la ensalada |
| pen | el bolígrafo | sandwich | el emparedado |
| pencil | el lápiz | scale | la báscula |
| penguin | el pingüino | scarf | la bufanda |
| pig | el cerdo | schoolbus | el autobus escolar |
| pillow | la almohada | school | la escuela |
| pink | rosa | scissors | la tijera |
| pizza | la pizza | scooter | el patinete |
| plate | el plato | seasons | las estaciones |
| police car | la patrulla | seven | siete |
| popcorn | las palomitas | shampoo | el champú |
| pot | la olla | shapes | las formas |
| potatoes | las patatas | sheep | la oveja |
| pull | tirar | ship | el buque |
| purple | violeta | shirt | la camiseta |
| purse | la cartera | shoes | los zapatos |
| push | empujar | shoulder | el hombro |
| quiet | tranquilo | shower | la ducha |
| rabbit | el conejo | sink | el lavabo |
| rain | la lluvia | sister | la hermana |
| rainbow | la arco iris | sit | sentarse |
| read | leer | six | seis |
| rectangle | el rectángulo | skateboard | el monopatín |
| red | rojo | skating | el patinaje |
| refrigerator | la nevera | skirt | la falda |
| rice | el arroz | sleeping | dormir |
| rocket | el cohete | snail | el caracol |
| rooster | el gallo | snake | la serpiente |
| ruler | la regla | sneakers | los tenis |
| running | correr | snow | la nieve |
| sad | triste | soap | el jabón |
| sailing | la vela | soccer | el fútbol |

# English-Spanish Word List

| | | | |
|---|---|---|---|
| **socks** | los calcetines | **ten** | diez |
| **soft** | suave | **tennis racket** | la raqueta de tenis |
| **spaghetti** | el espagueti | **three** | tres |
| **sponge** | la esponja | **tiger** | el tigre |
| **spoon** | la cuchara | **tights** | las mallas |
| **sports** | los deportes | **tissue** | el pañuelo |
| **spring** | primavera | **toast** | el pan tostado |
| **square** | el cuadrado | **toilet** | el inodoro |
| **squirrel** | la ardilla | **toilet paper** | el papel higiénico |
| **stairs** | las escaleras | **tomato** | el tomate |
| **standing** | de pie | **toothbrush** | el cepillo de dientes |
| **stapler** | la grapadora | **toothpaste** | la pasta de dientes |
| **star** | la estrella | **tornado** | el tornado |
| **stomach** | el estómago | **towel** | la toalla |
| **stool** | el taburete | **tractor** | el tractor |
| **stove** | la estufa | **train** | el tren |
| **strawberries** | las fresas | **transportation** | la transportación |
| **strong** | fuerte | **triangle** | el triángulo |
| **student** | la estudiante | **truck** | el camión |
| **submarine** | el submarino | **turkey** | el pavo |
| **summer** | el verano | **turtle** | la tortuga |
| **sun** | el sol | **two** | dos |
| **sunglasses** | las gafas de sol | **uncle** | el tío |
| **surprised** | sorprendido | **underwear** | la ropa interior |
| **sweater** | el suéter | **up** | arriba |
| **sweatshirt** | la sudadera | **walking** | caminar |
| **swimsuit** | el traje de baño | **wardrobe** | el armario |
| **table** | la mesa | **watermelon** | la sandía |
| **talking** | hablar | **weather** | el clima |
| **teacher** | el profesor | **wet** | mojado |
| **teapot** | la tetera | **whale** | la ballena |
| **television** | el televisor | **whisk** | el batidor |

# English-Spanish Word List

| | |
|---|---|
| whisper | susurrar |
| whistle | el silbato |
| white | blanco |
| wind | el viento |
| window | la ventana |
| winter | invierno |
| wolf | el lobo |
| wrist | la muñeca |
| yellow | amarillo |
| young | joven |
| zebra | la cebra |

Published by Dylanna Press an imprint of Dylanna Publishing, Inc.
Copyright © 2020 by Dylanna Press

Editor: Julie Grady

Printed in the U.S.A.

Printed in the USA
CPSIA information can be obtained
at www.ICGtesting.com
LVHW071524061023
760360LV00007B/18

9 781647 900120